THOUGHT CATALOG BOOKS

2 AM

2 AM

THOUGHT CATALOG

THOUGHT CATALOG BOOKS

Brooklyn, NY

THOUGHT CATALOG BOOKS

Copyright © 2016 by The Thought & Expression Co.

All rights reserved. Published by Thought Catalog Books, a division of The Thought & Expression Co., Williamsburg, Brooklyn. Founded in 2010, Thought Catalog is a website and imprint dedicated to your ideas and stories. We publish fiction and non-fiction from emerging and established writers across all genres. For general information and submissions: manuscripts@thoughtcatalog.com.

First edition, 2016

ISBN 978-1530629190

10 9 8 7 6 5 4 3 2 1

Cover photography by © Anunturi gratuite

Contents

1.	Yes, I Do Look Tired And Here's Why —*Ari Eastman*	1
2.	What If I'm Incapable Of Falling In Love Again? —*Kendra Syrdal*	5
3.	Love Like You've Been Hurt —*Heidi Priebe*	9
4.	Here's How To Stop Loving Them —*Ari Eastman*	13
5.	I Would Rather Wait An Eternity For You To Love Me Back Than Love Another —*Tyler Knott Gregson*	17
6.	I Still Dream About You —*Marisa Donnelly*	23
7.	I'm So Afraid That I'm Unworthy Of Your Love —*Bianca Sparacino*	25
8.	When The One You Could Love Forever Slips Away —*Beau Taplin*	27
9.	Me And My Monkey Brain —*Chrissy Stockton*	31
10.	26 Ways To Take Your Life Back When You're Broken —*Heidi Priebe*	35
11.	You're Not A Failure At Love Because You're Heartbroken —*Nicole Tarkoff*	45
12.	Why They Leave When They Still Love You —*Bianca Sparacino*	49

13.	What If Hearts Were Made To Be Broken? —*Rania Naim*	53
14.	What I Really Wish I Could Say To My Exes —*Kara Nesvig*	57
15.	I Hope The Way They Treated Your Love Haunts Them Forever —*Nikita Gill*	61
16.	You Have To Figure Out How To Save Yourself —*Alexandria Brown*	65
17.	The Last Time I Saw You Still Breaks My Heart —*Carly Dedrick*	69
18.	This Is How You Will Get Better After Being Broken —*Becca Martin*	71

1
Yes, I Do Look Tired And Here's Why

Ari Eastman

It's 12:52 AM on a Tuesday. The club is not going up. I'm clicking on a new thing every two seconds.

Click. Click. Click.

My brain works in morse code, trying to piece together my own incoherency when everyone else is too busy soaking up sleep. The messages stop. The texts cease. So it's just me.

I'm typing patterns with my own fingers. *Click.* Stop. *Click.* Stop. I'm lonely. *Click.* Stop. I'm not sure what's wrong. *Click.* Stop. I need to go back to therapy. *Click.* Stop. I can't afford what they're going to tell me. *Click.* Stop.

I do the usual rounds: Twitter, Facebook, Email, YouTube. Look at my phone at Snapchat. He's looked at my Snap. No text though. I reached out for help, and he ignored it. Funny, I think. He told me he was an asshole. Should have believed it.

Click. Think about how foolish I'm becoming. Or maybe more brave. I'm filtering myself less and less. Does this mean I'm learning to love myself? Does this mean I'm taking charge of my own truth? Or am I an asshole in artists' clothing? I cringe as I predict a comment: *"HA, she called herself an artist."*

Click.

I think about this insomnia, how it continues getting worse and worse. What little slumber I fall into is sporadic, interrupted every few hours and I realize that's all it's been. But at least my dreams stay vivid, so full of color, I can almost taste them. I feel so light, even as I'm chasing after broken promises and shadows that I can never reach. It feels good, when I'm finally asleep.

Click.

I know this sleep cycle means something needs my attention and I'm ignoring it. It eats away at me, but instead I'll eat something else. My feelings. Distracting myself with whatever I can consume. Media. Media. Media. I'm too busy *Click. Click. Clicking* on everything. Distraction is always in conjunction with depression, nipping at it's heels. Even now as I type this, *Gilmore Girls* is playing softly in the background. A separate window of Netflix, minimized. I keep trying to minimize everything. Fit it smaller and smaller. More screens. More distractions.

Something hurts, so I get up and eat. I'm not hungry. But I'm hurting and maybe I just want this hurt to be something I can easily fix. How cliche, trying to numb emotions with a box of cookies. I can't even be original in my sadness. I'm a living, breathing Tumblr blog. *Click.* Tumblr.

I'm always searching for something, but I never know what for. Click back on Twitter. Smile at something someone said. Try to savor this weird moment of social interaction. I think of the last time I actually looked someone in the eyes. Realize I talk to people all day, but haven't socialized in a while. Did I even leave my room? I don't answer my own question.

I start to rub my temples, a headache that I can't ever seem to kick. I could say it's from this blue screen. Oh, that glowing blue screen.

The internet, this vast plane of potential and heartbreak. Unlimited creativity and a breeding ground for hatred. What a place. And really, it's done so much for me. It's connected me to beautiful people, created real friendships, jobs, career starters. A place for a voice to be heard, even if I'm the only one under the assumption people are listening.

Click. I start to think of the different ways the internet has directly impacted my life.

Facebook, how that one boy came crawling back into my mouth and arms after months when we found each other in tagged photos. Twitter, where a photo of a cute boy with thick rimmed glasses turned into a real boy with thick rimmed glasses and eager hands that undid my bra. YouTube, the place it all changed. Melodramatic, sure. But the internet is a place I love so very much.

But do I love what it has done for me more than I actually love myself? I don't answer this question either. The headache sits in the back of my skull. Perhaps staring at anything too long can make you sick.

Distraction, it's what I do all day long. Finding ways to avoid the problems. Avoiding conversations. Avoiding the mirror when I pass by. I like the way I look, most days. I feel good in my own skin, despite the scars from the past.

But when I stop clicking and really take a look, I'm shocked at my reflection.

Someone else is looking back at me. I've been so distracted, I've forgotten who I even am.

Click.

2

What If I'm Incapable Of Falling In Love Again?

Kendra Syrdal

If you didn't know better, you'd think I never slept.

I am always one foot out the door right after we finish. I am always pulling my shirt on, tossing my hair up, and thinking, "I will worry about that later" in regards to getting home right after we fuck. I laughed out loud at that scene in *Trainwreck* where Amy Schumer boldly walk-of-shamed on a ferry but internally cringed because I've been there. Literally. I've been the girl in last night's cat eye and swollen "Please kiss away the pain" lips wishing she still smoked on the deck of the water taxi.

Because I'd rather freeze on the 30-minute ride back to the city with no jacket then dare to snuggle up next to someone overnight and humanize them.

If you didn't know better, you'd think I have never been infatuated.

I am always rolling my eyes about *The Notebook*, claiming that Noah and Amy (was her name Amy too?) should have taken more time apart because then maybe no one would have had to waste their time building some stupid house. I am the girl that everyone warned you about. The one who "functions like a guy" who "doesn't get attached" and will inevitably "break your heart without even meaning to." I don't understand people who can say the L Word without mapping it out, without mulling it over for weeks, months, even years.

Because I would rather swallow my tongue whole than say something before thinking about how it may be heard.

If you didn't know better you would think I wanted to be single.

I am content doing my own thing, being my own person. I do not get jealous at girls with boyfriends or find the idea of ANOTHER wedding invite tedious. I'm fiercely and unapologetically independent. I do what I want, when I want, and I only worry about the consequences when and if I need to. I love being responsible for me and only me. I don't think about what someone else is doing and why they are not involved in my life and that's okay.

Because I'd rather be sleeping alone than be responsible for someone else.

If you didn't know any better, you'd think I was emotionally dead inside.

And you know what? I don't know better and I think you might be right.

2 AM

I use people. I march to the beat of my own drum and do not worry about feelings because I'd rather they not exist. It is easier for me to just get exactly what I want from people and then drop them because if I keep them around, I will break when they drop me. So I keep them as far away as possible and pretend like I don't give a shit if they text me back because obviously, I do not care.

But really, I want to care. I want to be the person that they think about before they drift off to sleep at 1:30 AM. I want my phone to light up with notifications that will in turn make me smile. I want to *want* to spend the night, to graze my fingers affectionately across someone's back, to be the girl who is open and loves without abandon, but instead of I'm the girl who is leaving without so much as a goodbye.

I want to care; I just have stopped for so long that the feeling is now too foreign. It bites at me like when you can't remember the name of an actress being interviewed on E!. It sits at the back of my teeth and in the pit of my stomach like when you want to follow up the inevitable, "We need to talk" but do not know where to start. I want to verbalize what I'm feeling, but instead I'm apologizing for overstaying my welcome even though I have been invited in to make myself at home.
If you didn't know any better, you would think I gave zero fucks, but really I just do not want to be the one giving too many.

I say that I'm emotionally damaged. I joke that the part of my brain that releases oxytocin has gone on a permanent sabbatical. I nod along when people tote the, "You just haven't met the right person" banner while I silently disagree.

Because I'd probably even run from the right person.

If you didn't know better, you'd say that I run away from love.

And you're right; I'm just hoping that one day someone will chase me.

3

Love Like You've Been Hurt

Heidi Priebe

Love like you've been hurt.

Love like you've been let down, seen the other side of passion, come to understand that what can swell and expand and enlighten can also break down, fall to pieces, and destruct. Love like you know it isn't magic. That what can begin can also end, and that loving someone else is never going to be without that risk.

Love like you have been hopeless – like you have doubted love would ever come back to you, that your heart would ever heal, that passion and sincerity and mutual intoxication would ever be something you would get to hold inside your heart. Love like you've spent a lifetime working on yourself outside of love, because you know that you're the only person who will ever make you whole.

Love like you are braver now. Love like you're more compassionate. Love in a way that shows you understand other people have limits and issues and that you are not exempt from their overflow. Love in a way that knows that even the best of

people are going to fuck up and let you down and be entirely fallible and it's possible to keep loving them anyway. Love in a way that shows forgiveness where it is deserved.
Love like you understand – that if you don't keep trying to win them, every second of every passing day, you're going to lose them.

Love as though you've watched everything that you once wanted slip between your fingers and you remember what it felt like when it all crumbled apart. Love like someone who understands that it takes work to keep love alive. And you are somebody, now, who is willing to put in that work.

Love like you have been broken. Like your delusions have been crushed and your dreams have come undone and you have feared that you will never make it back to a place of trust and peace. Love like you know the deepest, murkiest, muddiest corners of love and you aren't afraid to go there again. Love like you know that it is worth it.

Because it is.

Because now, more than ever, you understand that love is not a miracle. It's not a mirage. It's not a drug that you're allowed to get hooked on and bleed another person dry from, always trying to get your next fix.

Love like you are patient. Like you're kinder. Like you're calmer and older and more understanding of what it takes to keep love alive in a world that does everything it possibly can to tear people apart from each other.

2 AM

Love like you've been deeply, irreparably hurt.

Because you'll be a better lover for it.

Because once you've been hurt, you know that it can happen again. That it may even be likely to. That your life is not a fairytale and your lover is not a God and that the decision to devote yourself to someone is inherently laden with risk.

And yet you're willing to take that risk anyway.

Because you are not falling in love this time, so much as you are walking headfirst into it. Choosing it. Accepting all the risk and the unknowns and deciding that it is worth it anyway.

Because that kind of love is ferocious.

And it makes each heartbreak before it worthwhile.

4

Here's How To Stop Loving Them

Ari Eastman

When you decide to stop loving them, your body will convince you this is the wrong decision. Everything inside burns with promises, with ideas about the future, with a different you. The you before the shattering. Before the ending. Before you were faced with the strangling thought that now, you are not supposed to love them anymore. Now, you are supposed to move on from this feeling.

Open up a box with all the memories you're trying to forget. Scatter them across the entire room, taking your time to not miss a single moment. Sit with all of it. Wonder if you can still smell someone on a shirt you haven't worn in so many moons. Do not run to the bottle or cell phone, ready to send messages you'll regret when the melancholy isn't aching so loudly. Just sit there.

Remember how it felt when they kissed your clavicle, or how their laugh always reminded you of a stampede. Wildebeest herd be damned, you'd risk being trampled every time.

Think about the first time your heart told you this feeling was different from before. It wasn't the love you'd heard of. This is the kind that bubbles up, an unwatched pot of water ready to explode. There is a power in it you cannot turn down.

Silently curse it. And then, verbally curse it. Look at all these ghosts of happier times and think how no one warned you of the leftover haunting. Saying goodbye doesn't mean everything ends.

Feel dirty, ashamed, like you should be better than this. Like you should know how to be okay. But you're not. So, yell. Yell to no one and everyone.
Pick out your favorite memory. The one that fills you with an ethereal glow, a warmth no fireplace or glass of wine could ever replicate. It's a full body feeling. Remember the purity in your happiness. Pin this memory to your chest and put the rest of them back in the box.

Store the box away. If it feels right, maybe you'll throw it out entirely. Just let it be out of sight right now.

Feel for your pulse. Marvel that every day, your heart beats about 100,000 times. It feels like you think of them 100,000 times. But your heart is still beating and pumping. Even though it feels broken, it's still going. And so are you.

Watch a movie or comedy special that forces laughter from your lips. One of those strong belly type laughs can send 20% more blood flowing, so giggle even when you aren't sure you can. Watch Aziz Ansari, or Amy Schumer, or John Mulaney, pick your favorite. Feel hearty bellows healing your body.

2 AM

Remember your heart is not broken. Broken things do not continue working. You are bruised. But you still *work*.

Call or reach out to someone who has always been there for you — a friend or family member. Tell them five different reasons they matter to you and how much you value your relationship with them. Sip on some nostalgia and joke about a story from your past together. Romantic love, while beautiful, is only *one* kind of love, and never enough to fully sustain a person. Take note of all the people you have in your life. All the love you have surrounding.

Go for a walk and make yourself a promise for the duration of your walk. *I will allow myself to feel whatever I feel.* And listen. With every step, check in with yourself. Are you sad? Are you angry? Do you feel utterly lost? Listen to all of it. Accept all of it. Decide this walk will be the time you finally let yourself off the hook. Decide this walk will be when you are allowed to grieve however you need.

Cry. Question. Break and look them up on social media. Want to cry more. Think of calling them. Of texting. Don't.

When you decide to stop loving them, you will do everything you can think of to make it come true. But maybe you aren't ready to stop. Maybe time, distance, or some other magic ingredient will do the trick. Or maybe, just maybe, it's okay to still love them. Perhaps your heart has enough room for some piece of love to stay forever. A preserved painting. An artifact of what you shared. An echo in the back of your chest. You will figure it out.

And if after all this, you still find yourself loving them, so what? We could all use more love, even if it's the type to be tucked away in a box.

5

I Would Rather Wait An Eternity For You To Love Me Back Than Love Another

Tyler Knott Gregson

I'd rather live an eternity in the purgatory of your love than one day in the hell of anyone else's. I would rather lie to myself every hour of every single day that I still have a chance, a hope, a prayer and a whisper of a promise at holding you and feeling you fall asleep lying on my chest than swallow the honest and choking pill that I will most likely die alone watching you smile in photos I will not be in and live a life I will have no part of. That you will grow, your hair will turn to snow and more than you'll come you'll go and I will stand and wait and wonder if you will discover that the fire I lit is still hot inside you.

How do I tell you what it feels like to know that you, You, have always been so much that happiness without you is a statistical impossibility, that once I met you my heart left my chest and flew directly into yours. Through your ribcage and it lives there now, where it will always live.

How do I express the pain that comes with knowing that you were and are and always will be that much, but I wasn't, and am not, and never will be enough to be those things to you? That you can find happiness in arms that are not mine and find passion in lips that are not connected to my face, that do not whisper the words that I have inside me?

How do I fall asleep and wish to wake up each morning knowing I was never enough to make you see a life with me, when I saw and wrote and prayed and never stopped believing in it every moment since our eyes found one another.

Would you listen if I explained that we are magic and that magic is something that doesn't require belief to be real, but requires that we make it day in and day out and maybe, just maybe, true magic is the disappearance of two people and the triumphant reemergence with great fanfare and the twirl of a red cape, of one new person instead?

Why is the ONE person that hurts us so badly the ONE person that we so sincerely need to sprint back to when all we need is a tiny breath of relief, a moment of feeling better? Why was I not ever enough to make you see what I see, to help you believe in me as I believed in you?

I am lost beyond the use of maps and stars. I will whisper to you like you can still hear me, I will speak softly across the emptiness and trick myself into thinking you are listening. I will carry you with me and see the world through our eyes instead of my own. I will love you until I die, and then I will start over and love you again, and then when that next light comes I will start fresh and give you more.

Each time through, each heartbreaking lap around this track we so foolishly named Life I will love you, no matter how happy you claim to be with someone else, no matter how much you think that convincing yourself that even though we are not it, we cannot Be it, will make all this go away, I will be there, loving you breathlessly and giving you all I have.

I will sacrifice all I am and drip the blood of my promise on the soil and the earth you stand upon. Perhaps I will begin the slow and painstaking practice of kissing all the glasses and mugs in the cabinets of your home. I will press my lips to their rims and I will leave silently knowing that at some point each and every day, your lips will be touching something that my lips were touching and in that fluttering moment, we were kissing once again.

If we were children again, made young and naive and blind to the way things just might turn out, would you run away with me? Would you pack your mom's smallest suitcase and fill it with your favorite clothes but mostly things to eat and the toys you couldn't bear to leave behind and run off into everywhere with me? The one great adventure of our lives and we'd share it together?

If I made you a book and I made me a book and titled them both "The Things I Did Not Say," do you understand that my book would hold only one word, a single word on all those hundreds of perfectly crisp pages of white. That on the final page, the only word I did not say through all this would be Goodbye. Would yours hold ink? Would the pages bleed through into each other? Would they look like a watercolor painting of the night sky with too little water and too few stars?

What if I was wrong? What if this too shall not pass and what if I should not amor my fati? Should I scratch them from my skin and call them liars and every single moment of every single day stare at the scars where they once lived and feel shame that I believed all this was one great push towards some final happiness?

Do I dare? Do I dare my love, speak up and say all the things you don't want me to say? Do I dare tell you Do Not Go. If Going means leaving and leaving means finding yourself in strange cities or stranger countries without my hand to hold through it all? Do I dare tell you to be with me, BE WITH ME, when I know you will close your eyes and without even entertaining the thought that we could and would be happy, say back to me, as if an automatic response, I Can't. Do I dare care, when caring is tearing me into tiny shreds of the man I used to be?

Do I tell you to stay with me, to be with me and trust me that what we are is worth taking the leap for and blending the rest of our lives from two into one? Do I dare tell you to love me for the rest of your days and stop pretending that the Knowledge of love is enough to carry me through the darkness of the rest of my life?

It's not, LOVE is enough, but love is giving and not saying, it's making and not imagining, it's holding and not wishing. Love is the reach, not the desire to do so. Love is the kiss not the regretting you cannot. Love is what we give and how we are to the person we love.

How do I tell you, tell you now that Love, true love is a Verb, not a noun that we capitalize to assign more worth that we thought it needed. Love is a verb, it's an action, do I dare tell you to use it wisely on me? I am already ready to hear that you can't, but I will wait until the day you can. As I said and I will say again, I would rather spend an eternity in the purgatory waiting for your love than a single burning day in the Hell of anyone else's.

6

I Still Dream About You

Marisa Donnelly

If you're wondering, yes. I still dream about you.

Not every single night, but it's always unexpected. Always when I tuck the covers under my chin and pull the pillows behind my back like a fortress keeping me safe; always when I close my eyes with other thoughts on my mind.

I dream about you in all the ways I remember you—with your hair chopped short, in your parents' house, at that outside restaurant in northern California, in your messy bedroom with the puppy curled between us, watching TV.

Sometimes you're the same, stubborn and distant, and I'm trying to decipher the expression on your face. Sometimes you're completely different, grabbing my hand and turning it over in yours like it's something you've never seen, pulling me to you, sliding closer to me in the diner booth.

In some dreams, we're in places I've never been. Rooms with tile floors and beach views, basements with cobwebs and no windows, busses to unknown destinations and neither of us are driving, distracted by one another's eyes, even when the tires are spinning and we're flying around corners.

Sometimes we talk. Sometimes we don't say anything. But we kiss. Then I wake up with my heart beating and my hands sweating and the blankets wrapped around my legs and my mind still spinning from the taste of your lips.

Yes, I still dream about you. Then I wake to the silence of my bedroom and mixed feelings, anger and sadness and longing swirling around my heart. And I wonder what you're dreaming, miles away, blankets and sheets and bedrooms away, if you're even sleeping. And then, before I roll over and drift away again, I ask the question I'll never know the answer to: *why.*

7
I'm So Afraid That I'm Unworthy Of Your Love

Bianca Sparacino

"I wish I had met you before I became myself." I said.

"What do you mean?"

And like that I was confessing my greatest insecurities, my greatest fears: "It is just…people always talk about the fact that your past builds you — that it influences the way you are and how you love and how you interact with the world you live in. When I say I wish I had met you before I became myself, I'm saying that I wish I had met you before heartbreak convinced me that I was safer on my own. I wish I had met you before I was walked out on four years ago, before my parents got divorced, before my little sister let someone break her teeth on promises. I wish I had met you before everything burrowed inside of me, before it all grew me into this person who may never feel worthy of loving a man like you."

He unlaced his fingers from my palms and pulled my face close to his. I could see saltwater dancing around his eyes, illuminated by the ashen shadow of the moon. I had never seen him cry and through the tears he said to me:

You don't see it do you? The beautiful battlefield you are. You come to me with your failed relationships and your stinging regrets, cupped within your hands, offered to me like an apology.

But, the thing is, you don't have to apologize for the way the world broke you. You don't have to ask me to forgive you for having scars, or doubts, or fears. You think you aren't enough, that your experiences took from you and left you lacking, but that couldn't be more wrong. Your past may have built you but it never reduced you, it never spoiled your potential — it only ever added to it, it only ever made you stronger, more deserving of a love that loves you back.

Sometimes my chest sinks into my stomach when I realize you truly don't see yourself the way I see you. See, I don't see your parents divorce, or your sisters despair. I don't see anguish stamped along your skin, I don't notice the tremble in your "I love yous." When I see you, I see roses. I see forests of potential just budding from your limbs. When I see you I see courage; I see a woman who is loving despite being afraid, I see a woman who is fighting despite feeling weak. When I see you I see a strength that inspires me.

He pressed his lips into mine, the power of his words filling my bones with warmth, and just like that I knew, that this man was a light in my life, and I would only ever want to grow towards him.

8

When The One You Could Love Forever Slips Away

Beau Taplin

To my sweetheart, my teacher, and kindred spirit.

What a senseless fool I have been and how ashamed I am for allowing you to slip away, for letting my past stand in the way of something so extraordinary, present and sincere. But this isn't a time for excuses or apologies. Heaven knows you have heard enough these last few weeks and I am now out of ways to express the enormous regret I feel and acknowledge that admitting to, or apologizing for my actions and mistakes does not make amends for them. Neither would I have you believe that this is a desperate plea to win back your affections. I am tired and ashamed of dampening your days with my desperate pressing and I never intend to do so again. Rather, I am writing you because anything else would be insincere. I am writing you because I adore you and nothing can be done about it. I am writing you because there are things that must be said and I can think of nothing else but you.

I remember, with every available minute, how soft and simple the days were with you. How each one fell gently into the arms of the next and instead of feeling trapped or anxious thinking ahead to the future, I wished, for the very first time in my life, that time would begin to slow down. That things would stay sweet and gentle, as they were, and that I would never taint or make a mess of all that was free and joyful in us.

You have always been someone I have respected enormously. Your mind is extraordinary, and the way you perceive the world around you with such enthusiasm and wonder moves me to do the same. I am so proud of all that you do, and all that you are. And the pleasure of seeing you apply yourself and achieve such spectacular heights motivates the people around you to push and fight harder for their own wishes and dreams.

There is never a dull moment with you. You move me to be more present and in tune with the world around me, and have a manner of making even the most mundane thing utterly magic and unforgettable. Every day with you has been a pleasure and a gift, and my god, you have made me happy and whole. You captivate me with your passions and send me positively mad with want and need. I want to roll around with you on the floor. See you dance and turn in the low light. Push my lips to that devilish grin again. Feel my hands on your hands and everywhere else. You make me wild and naive and a single kiss from you is enough to send me to ecstasy. You have this extraordinary energy about you that consumes and calms me all at once, and the way you dismantle my defenses and challenge me at every turn helps me to become a stronger and more passionate person. I feel capable of anything around you—you bring out my best self.

I love you, precious. It has been a privilege to love you. It is a privilege to love you. And though every day without you is agony and things between us have become messy and painful, there is a relief in knowing, at last, with absolute certainty, precisely what it is I want. I would like you to know that not a single day will go by where I would not give the world, and my very best, to make amends, to shelter and serve you, and know the immeasurable privilege of having your heart and trust with me once more. I adore you. You have been a true light in my life. And if nothing else, let these words speak to the profound and wonderful influence you have on the lives you touch. You certainly did on mine.

9

Me And My Monkey Brain

Chrissy Stockton

> *The thing under my bed waiting to grab my ankle isn't real. I know that, and I also know that if I'm careful to keep my foot under the covers, it will never be able to grab my ankle.*
> *– Stephen King*

One of the most incredible things about the human body is the endurance, quickness and creativity my brain exhibits in finding something new to be worried about. In this arena, it's never had an off day, never called in sick, never given me the reprieve of having a holiday. It is a slick machine, in this regard only.

We are descended from hunters who were also hunted. The things that should make us run stand out more than the things that should make us feel safe. It's not anything to feel bad about. It's just how we are wired.

I used to worry that I wouldn't find a job as a writer and when

I did I became worried I wouldn't write anything worth reading. One worry replaced the other seamlessly.

When my uncle died young and suddenly I became obsessed with the idea that I would too. *I have a heart murmur, I am out of shape, my pulse is 84 and I have been laying down for 27 minutes and Google says it should be lower* — I could list a lot of proofs for this theory that I've gathered in the middle of the night, when my little detective brain likes to be most active.

I went to the doctor and cried in her office because the weight of holding onto this worry was drowning me. I think she wanted to laugh because – and here's the thing, even from my perspective I can see this – these thoughts were irrational. But she said we could do tests anyway, if I wanted. I took my shirt off and she connected little sticky dots to me and I laid down while she looked for something dangerous or abnormal.

When she told me I was fine and healthy, do you think I breathed some big sigh of relief?

The recurring pattern is this: something makes me nervous. Something is the scratching post for my anxiety. Without ever meaning to, I orient my life around it. What I do, what I avoid, there's a magnetic pull around whatever this THING happens to be at the time.

And then critical mass. And then I figure it out. And then I find the strength to get over it, to shine a flashlight into the dark and realize the monster isn't there.

And then I think there should be some kind of relief, a victory lap to celebrate the miracle of confrontation. Or *something*. I should get to laugh and move on. But there is a new closet with a new monster that somehow seems real even though I have a lifetime of experience in knowing that they never are.

I had a yoga teacher who called this monkey brain. It's a buddhist concept, Chitta Vrittis, the busy, cluttered, scattered thoughts that litter a mind you are trying to organize and focus. The answer they say, harder in execution than in identification, is to acknowledge each bit of mental chatter as it crosses your mind. Confrontation, not resistance.

I don't know what that means in real life. I'm here. I have a new worry in the dark. My brain is doing what my brain is supposed to do and looking for predators. It doesn't want me to brush all these threats off, it wants me to survive and in what kind of quality is an afterthought. Evolution has breed me to be a hunter, not a yogi.

10

26 Ways To Take Your Life Back When You're Broken

Heidi Priebe

There's an old, outdated assumption that time heals all wounds. But I believe this to be untrue. In the words of Dr. Phil, "*Time doesn't change us. It's what we do with that time that changes us.*" We are all more than capable of taking control back into our own hands when life knocks us down. It's just a matter of doing so deliberately. Of making changes that will move us forward. Of finding a way to progress with purpose, rather than simply letting life knock us around into whoever we will become next. When you're feeling lost and disheartened with life, here are 26 simple methods of taking your power back.

1. Get In Shape.

Strong bodies and strong minds go hand-in-hand. Forget about how your workout routine is making you look and start focusing on how it makes you feel – on the strength, the dedication and the structure that it brings to your mindset. By harnessing your physical power, you're reminding yourself that you're capable of so much more than you used to be. In the words of Jillian Michaels, "*Fitness isn't about a crunch or a push up. It's about taking your power back.*"

2. Get out of town.

Take a day, a week or a month to escape your usual surroundings and welcome in the world outside your doorstep. Sometimes a change in mindset is as simple as a change in scenery – and being away from home allows you the space, the freedom and the tranquility to heal on your own terms.

3. Rewrite your story.

The past is nothing more than a story we repeat to ourselves – and allowing ourselves to understand this is an incredibly liberating notion. Visit a narrative therapist who can help you reframe your experiences, or journal them out until you're able to come to a new understanding of why things happened the way they did. Learn to pinpoint the opportunities for growth within the destruction of your past – and then move forward with those opportunities close to your heart.

4. Invite new people into your life.

The positive effect we are able to have on one another as humans is immeasurable. Sometimes the best way to heal from the toxicity of past relationships is to allow the beauty of new ones to flourish. We all end up thinking, behaving and being like the people we spend the most time around – so choose the ones who make you want to be the best possible version of yourself.

5. Tell your story.

Be honest about your past. Share the pain of everything that's happened to you and allow your strength in moving past it to inspire other people. Don't hide or downplay anything that feels important to you. Refuse to apologize for where you've been.

6. Be disciplined about self-care.

When we're sick, we take particular care to rest, drink fluids and take medicine – even if it temporarily impedes on our productivity. When we're struggling emotionally, we have to take care of ourselves in much of the same way. By making self-care a priority, you are setting yourself up for a quicker and infinitely less painful recovery.

7. Change your appearance.

Sometimes we need a deliberate outward change to reflect a subtle internal one. By altering your hair, makeup or style, you're concretely welcoming change into your life – and recognizing that it can be a good thing. In fact, it can even be something that happens on your own terms.

8. Quit what isn't working for you.

When the stakes are down and our lives are lying in shambles, we are paradoxically awarded the ideal opportunity to start over. Use your ill fortune as the excuse you've been waiting for to walk away from that shitty job, toxic relationship or commitment that is making you miserable. If you're going to be forced to start over, you might as well do it once, the right way.

9. Give yourself permission to let go.

Not everything that happens to us has to have a meaning or a lesson. If your past no longer serves you, give yourself permission to let go and forget about the pain that has been holding you back. You dictate your story and you don't have to place emphasis on anything that makes you feel small.

10. Connect with people who've been through something similar.

Seek out the words, company and comforts of those who understand what you're going through. Read their stories, cherish the wisdom they've gleaned and use it as a constant, pervasive reminder that you are never alone.

11. Unplug for an entire week.

If you are able to do so, take a full week of your life and spend it outdoors or on the road, somewhere where your Facebook notifications can't reach you. Sometimes it takes disconnecting from your everyday life to realize how trivial most of your worries are – and how capable you are of existing completely outside of them.

12. Physically de-clutter your life.

Take a full weekend to clean your apartment or home in a way that you never have before – ruthlessly ridding it of everything you no longer use and organizing it in a way that feels mentally refreshing. When our physical environments are in order, it becomes easier to keep our minds uncluttered, too.

13. Strengthen your relationships with the people who love you.

A close friend once told me "There's no time like when you're down on your luck to realize who's really there for you in life." When everything is falling apart, take notice of who is still standing beside you – those are the people who are always going to matter the most. And there's no time like the present to appreciate them for all they're worth.

14. Follow the food guide for a month.

Even the healthiest among us aren't always putting the right foods into our bodies. So for one month, try to do so. Eat the right amounts of fruits, veggies, grains, dairy and meat (or meat alternatives). Notice changes in your energy level and mindset – and then try it all over again the next month.

15. Take a course that teaches you something new.

What we know changes the landscape of who we are. By adding to your internal database of knowledge, you are expanding your horizons and reminding yourself that there is always more to be learned and always more ways for your worldview to shift.

16. Make a budget and stick to it.

It's difficult to feel in control of our lives when our finances are out of control. By coming face-to-face with our spending habits, we're giving ourselves a leg up on conquering them effectively. There's nothing quite as soothing as figuring out a way to live below your means.

17. Establish a healthy source of validation.

None of us are islands. Though we all strive to be strong, independent adults in our day-to-day lives, we all need love and affection. And finding a friend or loved one who is willing to remind you why you're wonderful when you forget it just might be what keeps you afloat on the bad days. Validation is not toxic if you're seeking it in the right places.

18. Become invested in the process of change, not the outcome.

Too often, we pit all of our hopes on future accomplishments that may never come to fruition. Rather than telling yourself

'*I'll be happy when…*' learn to find joy in the simple process of bettering yourself. Take pride in the fact that you're making changes for yourself, rather than pitting your happiness on the outcome of those changes.

19. Learn a new language.

Learning a new language may be one of the best available ways to remind yourself that there's an entire world out there – one that operates on a completely different premise than yours. Committing to learning a non-native language proves that you could adapt and mould to one of those other realities if you wanted to – which consequently makes you feel a little less defeated by yours.

20. Learn to walk away.

Perhaps the single most important step to regaining control over your life comes through learning to walk away from the situations that are holding you back. It takes an incredible amount of bravery to break away from what you've known. But it also gives way to an incredible opportunity to start over the way you've always wanted to.

21. Let yourself be happier than you are comfortable with.

Too often, we sabotage our own happiness out of a reluctance to trust it. Rather than allowing ourselves to grow into bigger shoes, we declare our feet 'not big enough' and retreat. We have to start allowing ourselves to let go of guilt and self-doubt and start seizing opportunities as they arise. Even if we feel a bit out of our league along the way.

22. Set and enforce boundaries.

There will eternally be people out there who are willing to rob you of your joy in exchange for a dose of their toxicity. And one of the most important lessons we may ever have to learn is that we cannot save those people from themselves. We have to learn to set clear boundaries if we don't want to drown alongside them. Even if it's someone we love.

23. Cut out a vice for 100 days.

The idea of never drinking, smoking or eating junk food again is an intimidating enough mission for any of us to give up on before we've even gotten started. So instead of resolving to cut out one of your vices eternally, try cutting one out for 100 days. It is enough time for you to see the positive effects of what you've done, but a short enough time for the end to always be in sight. And who knows – maybe once you realize how great you feel without one of your vices, it will turn into a permanent lifestyle change.

24. Try something that genuinely scares you.

There is nothing that boosts confidence quite like overcoming your fears. Make a deliberate point to take on a challenge that has always scared you when you're feeling down – though it may seem like ridiculous timing to do so, the strength and sense of self-efficacy that will come from conquering your worries will take you further than you could possibly imagine.

25. Look at how far you have come.

Look back at the person who was once so lost and then look at who you've become since then. You may not be all the way to where you'd like to be, but you're on your way. And you're a hell of a lot further than you used to be.

26. Forgive others. Forgive the Universe. Forgive yourself.

Don't allow anger or fear to keep you trapped in a damaging past. Allow yourself the opportunity to forgive those who have hurt you, to forgive the injustices done to you and to forgive yourself for everything you messed up on your path to redemption. Forgive not to relieve other people of accountability, but to finally allow yourself the freedom and space to move on. And to take your damn life back.

11

You're Not A Failure At Love Because You're Heartbroken

Nicole Tarkoff

There's no such thing as failing at love, there's only refusing to try. You fail when you allow fear to keep you comfortable.

Love isn't comfortable; it's scary. It's knowing there is someone out there who makes you feel like your life would fall apart without them, and it's living with the perpetual fear of that possibility.

And when that moment becomes reality you feel like you've been broken. You feel your life move forward, but you're walking through it facing backwards. One foot steps behind the other, instead of in front, and the past is a place you continue to retreat to, but when you lose some *thing* it's completely normal to retrace your steps, and losing some *one* is no different.

One thing that continues to pass is time, and whenever you're in pain you wish it would pass by faster.

And others will tell you that time heals all wounds, but you won't feel yourself recovering until one day you wake up and the scab is completely gone. But you didn't one day suddenly become better, it was a process that you were unaware was happening. Because sometimes you only realize you're healing until after you're healed.

And in the duration of this healing, when time feels slow and every day's a struggle, the only thing to do is cope. So you attempt to distract yourself in every way possible, with people, things, substances, anything that will keep your thoughts from filling the silence. And then you realize that distractions only occupy your mind for so long, and that's when the feeling of failure kicks in.

And failure turns into frustration because even if you succeed at everything else, the one place you want success to happen it won't. But heartbreak isn't failure, it's trial and error. It's a step taken toward something you thought was the right direction, but turned out to be wrong. And most times you don't automatically reroute. You wander and feel lost.

But the time you spent giving your heart to someone who broke it is just as valuable as the time it takes to heal. Because the time you devoted to learning about someone else resulted in you learning about yourself.

It isn't failure if you've become more aware of who you are and what you need; it would be failure to continue to settle for anything less.

2 AM

And suddenly you find yourself adjusting to a new way of life without the person who used to make you happy, but you shouldn't think of happiness as something that occurred in the past. Happiness is something you need to make room for in your future, and it needs to originate from a source within yourself. Don't attempt to make your life happier by finding someone. Find happiness and then find someone to share it with. And find the strength to risk heartbreak as a result.

Your broken heart is an indication that you have enough courage to give so much of yourself to someone that you get hurt in return. **You're not a failure at love because your heart is broken, you're a failure at love if you let the fear of heartbreak keep you from loving at all.**

12

Why They Leave When They Still Love You

Bianca Sparacino

They didn't leave you because they didn't love you. They left because when they were fourteen they had their best friend come to them with a heart that never healed. At fourteen they held a human being, trembling and broken in their paper arms, and they feared the day they would mourn a last goodbye, a last embrace. They left because they saw how a cold flame could create a house fire in the hollow bones of someone who gave every inch of themselves and still came up short.

No, they didn't leave you because they didn't love you. They left because when they were seventeen they finally noticed the distance between their parents at the dinner table. At seventeen they had to tell their younger brother, sister, that sometimes things get tough, that sometimes mistakes hang heavy in a ribcage and it causes people to run away. They left because at a tender age they were taught that "I love you" doesn't always mean, 'I'll stay.'

They didn't leave you because they didn't love you. They left because at twenty-one they read an article about a dating app that mentioned how 42% of its users already had partners. At twenty-one they read that plan b's and second options were always on the forefront, always in the back pocket of someone who was holding the hand of a man, a woman, who slept soundly beside them at night. They left because they convinced themselves that there would always be another, someone better suited, someone better looking, someone more successful; it would only ever be a matter of time.

See, they didn't leave you because they didn't love you. They left because at twenty-five they watched their grandfather empty out the oceans within him at the grave of his high school sweetheart. At twenty-five they watched how he slowly deteriorated, how loss crept into his heart like a bleak December frost; how the doctor said that her demise killed him before old age ever had the chance. They left because they finally understood, how cruel it truly was to love something that death could touch.

Trust me when I say, they didn't leave you because they didn't love you. They left you because they never learned that they could be better than their past. They left you because they couldn't convince themselves that they wouldn't turn into their parents, that they wouldn't wake up one day and want to flee. They left you because they never saw devotion win, they never saw passion triumph.

No, they didn't leave you because they didn't love you.

2 AM

They left you because they didn't love themselves enough to believe that they could be different.

13

What If Hearts Were Made To Be Broken?

Rania Naim

We often think of the pain that comes with heartbreak; the agony, the tears and the darkness that blinds us. We think of how it changes us, how it takes away the purest and most innocent parts of us. We think of all the days and nights we spent promising ourselves not to ever feel like this again or be that vulnerable again but then we find ourselves willingly walking through the fire once more, burning with every step we take.

We don't realize that we also break some hearts, and we inflict the same pain we are trying to avoid on others. We wreck people who only wanted to love us and we love people who only wanted to wreck us.

If you could go back and change your heartbreak, would you? And if you did, would that change make your life better? Will it make you happier? Or would that change conceal the scars that you pride yourself on? The scars that give you extra strokes of beauty.

If you knew for sure, the moment you were born that your

heart was made to be broken, would you still suffer when it breaks?

Without heartbreak, there is no struggle, and struggle makes us fight for our lives.

Without heartbreak, there are no lessons, and lessons teach us how to live.

Without heartbreak, there is no growth, and growth allows us to guide ourselves and others.

Without heartbreak, there are no questions, and questions open up our minds.

Without heartbreak, there is no faith, and faith gives us hope when there is none.

Without heartbreak, there are no tears, and tears wash away the pain.

Without heartbreak, there is no suffering, and suffering introduces us to compassion.

Without heartbreak, there is no darkness, and darkness leads us to light.

Without heartbreak, there is no healing, and healing re-awakens our love.

Without heartbreak, there is no change, and change renews the way we see the world.

2 AM

What if we glorified heartbreak? What if heartbreak was more like a minor bruise? Would we still take it so personally? Would we still struggle to heal or get out of bed? What if heartbreak was an optical illusion we keep misinterpreting?

Maybe our hearts were made to broken, maybe our hearts know that they can take more pain than we give them credit for. Maybe Rumi was right when he said "You have to keep breaking your heart until it opens." Maybe breaking our hearts is the only way to open them. And maybe after all these heartbreaks, love will finally find its way in.

14

What I Really Wish I Could Say To My Exes

Kara Nesvig

Dear Ex-Boyfriends,

Thanks for everything. Well, mostly everything. Thanks for being my boyfriends when I wanted you to be, for the glasses of wine and free dinners and laughs and shit like that. The further removed I am from you now, the more grateful I am for everything. I try really hard not to dwell on all the bad stuff – and believe me, with some of you, the bad stuff was pretty bad. But focusing on positive things makes you a better person, which is what I'm aiming for with these thank-you notes. I'll never actually send them in the mail, but it's the thought that counts, right? (And if they do appear in your mailbox, please arrange to have me committed.)

1. Thanks for all the wine, and the French fries at that little dimly-lit restaurant we loved so much. Thank you for understanding that I didn't want to make you a part of my social media life, but that you were incredibly important nonetheless. It's just that I like to keep my boyfriends away from that. I don't want my relationships played out over Instagram. Thank you for leaving me when I needed you most, for making me grieve in a very real way and learn how to wrap my mind around that grief. Thank you for never really cutting the cord that ties us together, for sleeping with me in Minnesota and New York City, kissing me exactly the same way you did when we fell in love. Thank you for breaking my heart not once but twice. I learned. I grew. I stood up on my own. Thank you for coming back.

2. Thank you for being the first, the sweet, tenderhearted farm boy I cut my teeth on. Thank you for teaching me how all this worked, for the phone calls that lasted for hours on our mid-2000s cell phones til the data ran out, for the countless kisses in a tractor cab and a beet truck. Thank you for squiring me to all those high school touchstones: homecoming dances, proms, football games. Thank you for being just the right guy for my teenage self and for being a dear friend now, regardless of our different lives.

3. Thank you for being the man I needed when I needed you, for being around to fill a void and for letting me go when you knew I was on my way out. Neither of us were right for the other, but it was fun while it lasted. I learned that "nice" isn't really what I'm looking for in a relationship, that "fine" isn't the right way to describe your boyfriend to your friends. You were kind and gentle and thoughtful, but you weren't the One.

4. I guess I still don't have a lot to thank you for. I'm still kind of smarting over this one, two years later. You can't have it all, you know. Some things are just tougher to move on from than others, and our hot-and-cold relationship is one of them. Was one of them. Thank you for giving me a whole novel full of stories to write about it. Thank you for that. Thank you for pushing me out of my comfort zone once we broke up; I had to leave a bunch of our friends behind and isolate myself for awhile, which turned out to be a good thing. Thanks for making me feel so horrible and heartbroken that all I could do was just write it out. Thanks for making me entertain the idea of moving to a completely different state just to get away from you, save up the money for it and ultimately decide against it. Thanks for dating a girl who is so pretty, nice and perfect that she gives me full-throttle panic attacks until I realize that she's totally normal too, and that you 100% were not the One for me, even though I wanted you to be so badly. So thanks – thanks for making me grow the fuck up and learn how to get over things. Thanks for making me trip and fall really hard and get back up on my own.

15

I Hope The Way They Treated Your Love Haunts Them Forever

Nikita Gill

I hope the way they treated your love haunts them forever. The way you poured your soul into them, the way you turned every darkness they had into light. The way you kissed their forehead when they were in pain and supported them through the most terrible times of their lives. May they long for you in the moments when they are looking for someone who loves them, who understands them, and can find no one who does it so well as you.

I hope the way they let you go haunts them forever. You deserved better than a text message, a phone call, a cold voice that had no more time to spend than a few seconds on you. You deserved better because you stayed up night after night to speak to them when they were in pain, travelled miles for them just to see them because they needed you that day. You deserved better from someone you trusted with your heart, who demanded your surrender and then left you for someone else, someone who they said was better. May their eyes always look away in shame when someone mentions your name.

I hope the way they dismissed your effort haunts them forever. The heartache that they put you through because their pride was more important, being right was more important to them than the way you felt about something. The amount of times that they were late and you forgave them because that is just what people who are deeply in love do. May they be treated the same way and remember that this was how they treated someone who once gave their heart and soul to them, someone who deserved better.

I hope that one day their ghost leaves your dreams and you aren't haunted by them forever. May your soul heal from the wounds they inflicted callously by treating your love like it meant nothing, ever. Repeat to yourself every night before you fall into that fitful sleep: *I deserved better than this. And I will love again.*

Because that is the truth, darling. That is the purest truth about you. You deserve someone who treats your love like it is more precious than anything else in the world. You deserve someone who looks at your effort and considers themselves fortunate for having someone who cares so much in *their* world.

I hope that you forget the way they treated you and someone else treats you a thousand times better. Your ability to love has been tested with fire and you may be burned, but you have come out alive despite all your tears. Your heart has been broken, but it is strong enough to mend. You have fallen in love before and you will fall in love again.

May the next person you fall in love with, treasure your heart the way it deserves and never breaks it or rips it at the seems. I hope the next person you love gives you all the respect, the love and the truth that you need.

16

You Have To Figure Out How To Save Yourself

Alexandria Brown

I think letting something go is probably one of the hardest things we all have to do eventually. I don't only mean with romantic relationships. It's hard to admit failure no matter what the situation is. There have been many times with friends, boyfriends and jobs that I have held on way longer than I should have.

But we all do that. Especially when it comes to love. As a natural born fighter, I've been the person trying to convince other people to love me since the day I came into the world. For some reason I have always thought that I had to almost trick someone into liking me because genuine love would never be something I'll get. I just wasn't the lovable kind. So I'd sell myself (not actually) to anyone who passed by in order to feel some kind of love.

The worst part was that I was always trying to convince myself to love me. Do you know how hard it is to sell something to the most resistant buyer in the world? If you know me at all you'll know that I have made some really terrible decisions when it comes to love.

It all stems from the fact that for a long time I couldn't love myself. Even now I struggle.

I've dated married men. Phew. That feels like a weight lifting. I've dated them because it was an ego boost. The worst kind of ego boost but it did the trick for a while. People often think because of this that either my dad wasn't around or my parents weren't good parents. Both of those things aren't true. I don't have dad issues, my mom is my best friend and my family is one of those good ones many people dream they have.

I think this is why people don't really understand why I made the decisions I made in the past. I was always good with being the girl who was around for a minute instead of a lifetime. Late night phone calls were the way I lived my life for a good portion of my 20s. It was as empty as it sounds but it also gave me a feeling of wholeness. How contradictory I know but it's true. It filled the need for ego but it didn't fill the role of love.

I've also realized that forced love is not love.

As much as we wish we could make the person we love turn around and love us right back, we can't. Would you really want someone you had to convince every day to love you or would you rather meet someone who just does?

Then it hit me, I didn't need to convince everyone else to love me, I needed to start loving me. I needed to start looking in the mirror and recognize myself as someone who deserves my love. I needed to start taking care of myself. There was nothing that someone else could give me that I couldn't give me. I needed to start to focus on fighting for myself.

Being broken doesn't mean unfixable. It means that you have to start somewhere and try to glue back the pieces. It's great if you have someone to help you but you know how the broken pieces fit together better than anyone.

You alone know how to make yourself feel whole.

17

The Last Time I Saw You Still Breaks My Heart

Carly Dedrick

When we woke up that morning,
I knew it would be the last time I saw you.

What I didn't know yet
Was how you would watch me from the corner,
As I pulled off your shirt
And pulled on my dress.

How when I would ask you for help with the buttons
That my hands couldn't reach,
You would sit up so quickly
And then take your time –

Like your fingers were saying goodbye
To each notch in my spine.
Like you were writing a resignation letter
Straight to my bones,
An apology for leaving half-finished,
A job that you just couldn't do anymore.

What I didn't know yet

Was how I would sit on your lap,
Press my face into your shoulder
And find nothing to say.

How stupid this would seem to me later
When I looked at myself in the mirror,
And could only see
All of the words that I had for you.

I didn't know yet
How I would wrap my hands around your head,
So I could feel the exact place
Where your hair met your neck.
Or how I would stop at the end of your stairs,
To wonder what would happen if I climbed back up them.

How for the longest time I would think of you
As my hardest goodbye,
Until someone else came along
Who would eventually steal all of your thunder.

What I couldn't have known yet
Was the way I would still remember you now:
Looking at me with your arm out the window,
And my name in your mouth –

How you didn't seem to mind as much as I did,
That it was the last time I would hear you say it out loud.

18

This Is How You Will Get Better After Being Broken

Becca Martin

You feel like you're suffocating, like your lungs don't work. You can barely gasp enough air in each breath to get any words out. You try to calm down but every time you get close the pain stings you again and you're right back to feeling like you're slowly dying. *Dying.* This has to be what dying feels like. You feel like you're drowning. Like someone put you six feet under, close enough to see the surface but never close enough to get to the top and be okay again. You feel like this is the end. The end of everything you've ever known, or everything you care to remember.

You just want everyone to stop asking if you're okay, because you're not. How could you possibly be okay? It feels like your heart was just ripped out of your chest and ran over by a truck, a big fucking truck. The pit in your stomach just grows and grows, as you are so sick of hearing people to tell you to eat. You don't want to eat. You're literally sick to your stomach and the last thing you care about is eating.

You have a million questions running through your head, but if he called you you don't know the first thing you'd say.

How could he hurt you this way? What did you do to deserve this? How could you all the sudden feel so unloved and unlovable?

Your trust is gone. It felt like it was just ripped away from you without warning, almost like the sharp pain of a paper cut slicing open your finger, but a million times worse. It's just gone, everything feels gone, and you feel exposed and raw. The wound feels so deep and you don't know if a hundred stitches could fix the mess your in.

Hate starts to fill your heart. You never imagined that you could feel anger and hate towards him like this. You didn't think he could ever do this to you. You expected so much more, but you were wrong. You were so, so wrong.

It doesn't feel real; everything feels like a dream like all you have to do is open your eyes and this nightmare will end. But it won't. You can't understand how he could do this to you. He loved you, right? Someone who loves you doesn't hurt you. At least not in this way. Playing too rough in a pick up basketball game is one thing; not calling you back is another, but this? How could you do this to you? How could he cheat on you?

With all this anger, all this hate, all this sadness and all this confusion that is engulfing your life right now I want you to know it won't always feel like this. I promise you it won't.

The tears that are running down your face like a faucet will slow down; they will slowly turn into a leaky faucet that only drips some times before it is fixed, maybe not completely, but enough to almost fix the problem. The weight that once manipulated you when you felt like you were being pulled six feet under will somehow, almost magically, start to dissolve and you will float to the top and breath normal again. You will start to feel like yourself again. Your appetite will come back and you will go out to eat with your friends again and you will laugh.

You will start to enjoy your freedom again. You will start to trust again. You will start to love again. Because you are not unlovable and you are not unworthy of someone treating you the way you deserve to be treated. And yes, you do deserve to be treated a certain way because you went through hell and fought your way back.

You didn't let a broken heart stop you, maybe temporarily, but you got back up in time.

Time heals all wounds they say, and I believe they're right for the most part. But I also know that you can't speed up time, no matter how much you wish it would go faster, no matter how bad you want the pain you're feeling to start fading away.

But it will get better, I promise you.

Thought Catalog, it's a website.
www.thoughtcatalog.com

Social
facebook.com/thoughtcatalog
twitter.com/thoughtcatalog
tumblr.com/thoughtcatalog
instagram.com/thoughtcatalog

Corporate
www.thought.is

Made in the USA
San Bernardino, CA
09 March 2019